CATS AND KITTENS
CHARTED DESIGNS

by Julie S. Hasler

DOVER PUBLICATIONS, INC.
NEW YORK

Copyright © 1986 by Julie S. Hasler.
All rights reserved under Pan American and International Copyright Conventions.

Published in Canada by General Publishing Company, Ltd., 30 Lesmill Road, Don Mills, Toronto, Ontario.
Published in the United Kingdom by Constable and Company, Ltd.

Cats and Kittens Charted Designs is a new work, first published by Dover Publications, Inc., in 1986.

Manufactured in the United States of America
Dover Publications, Inc., 31 East 2nd Street, Mineola, N.Y. 11501

Library of Congress Cataloging in Publication Data

Hasler, Julie S.
  Cats and kittens charted designs.

  (Dover needlework series)
  1. Cross-stitch—Patterns.   2. Needlework—Patterns.   3. Decoration and ornament—Animal forms.   4. Cats in art.   5. Dogs in art.   I. Title.   II. Series.
  TT778.C76H37   1986   746.44′041   85-25416
  ISBN 0-486-25071-7

Preface

Throughout history the cat has been used to symbolize everything from mystery and intrigue to innocence and playfulness. These thoroughly contradictory creatures, aloof and affectionate by turns, have long spurred people's imagination. Considered sacred in ancient Egypt, devils in the Middle Ages and treasured pets by children of any era, cats cast a spell that shows no signs of abating. Today, they are more popular than ever. Here is a selection of felines sure to please any cat fancier. From the mischievousness of a kitten playing with a ball of yarn, to the serenity of a pair of Redpoint Siamese, to highly stylized medallions, these designs capture the many facets of the cat's nature. The charts can be used to create pictures, pillows, rugs, afghans or other items to show your appreciation of these fascinating animals.

General Directions

Most of these designs were originally created for counted cross-stitch or needlepoint, but they are easily translated into other needlework techniques. Keep in mind that in counted-thread work, the finished piece will not be the same size as the charted design unless you are working on fabric or canvas with the same number of threads per inch as the chart has squares per inch. With knitting and crocheting, the size will vary according to the number of stitches per inch.

Many of the designs list a color for the background in the color key. If you are working the design in needlepoint, use the color listed; for cross-stitch, use fabric this color and leave the background stitches unworked. If no background color is listed, leave the background unworked on cross-stitch and use any color desired on needlepoint.

COUNTED CROSS-STITCH

MATERIALS

1. **Needles.** A small blunt tapestry needle, No. 24 or No. 26.

2. **Fabric.** Evenweave linen, cotton, wool, or synthetic fabrics all work well. The most popular fabrics are aida cloth, linen and hardanger cloth. Cotton aida is most commonly available in 18 threads-per-inch, 14 threads-per-inch and 11 threads-per-inch (14-count is the most popular size). Evenweave linen comes in a variety of threads-per-inch. To work cross-stitch on linen involves a slightly different technique (see page 4). Thirty thread-per-inch linen will result in a stitch about the same size as 14-count aida. Hardanger cloth has 22 threads to the inch and is available in cotton or linen. To determine the size of a cross-stitch design, divide the number of stitches in the design by the thread-count of the fabric. For example: If a design 112 squares wide by 140 squares deep is worked on a 14-count fabric, divide 112 stitches by 14 (=8), and 140 by 14 (=10). The design will measure 8″ × 10″. The same design worked on 22-count fabric measures about 5″ × 6½″.

3. **Threads and Yarns.** Six-strand embroidery floss, crewel wool, Danish Flower Thread, pearl cotton or metallic threads all work well for cross-stitch. DMC Embroidery Floss has been used to color-code the patterns in this volume; a conversion chart for Royal Mouliné Six-Strand Embroidery Floss from Coats & Clark and Anchor Embroidery Floss from Susan Bates appears on page 7. Crewel wool works well on evenweave wool fabric. Danish Flower Thread is a thicker thread with a matte finish, one strand equaling two of embroidery floss.

4. **Embroidery Hoop.** A wooden or plastic 4″, 5″ or 6″ round or oval hoop with a screw-type tension adjuster works best for cross-stitch.

5. **Scissors.** A pair of sharp embroidery scissors is essential to all embroidery.

PREPARING TO WORK

To prevent raveling, either whip-stitch or machine-stitch the outer edges of the fabric.

Locate the exact center of the chart (many of the charts in this book have an arrow at the top or bottom and side; follow these arrows to their intersection to locate the chart center). Establish the center of the fabric by folding it in half first vertically, then horizontally. The center stitch of the chart falls where the creases of the fabric meet. Mark the fabric center with a basting thread.

It is best to begin cross-stitch at the top of the design. To establish the top, count the squares up from the center of the chart, and the corresponding number of holes up from the center of the fabric.

Place the fabric tautly in the embroidery hoop, for tension makes it easier to push the needle through the holes without piercing the fibers. While working continue to retighten the fabric as necessary.

When working with multiple strands (such as embroidery floss) always separate (strand) the thread before beginning to stitch. This one small step allows for better coverage of the fabric. When you need more than one thread in the needle, use separate strands and do not double the thread. (For example: If you need four strands, use four separated strands.) Thread has a nap (just as fabrics do) and can be felt to be smoother in one direction than the other. Always work with the nap (the smooth side) pointing down.

For 14-count aida and 30-count linen, work with two strands of six-strand floss. For more texture, use more thread; for a flatter look, use less thread.

EMBROIDERY

To begin, fasten the thread with a waste knot and hold a short length of thread on the underside of the work, anchoring it with the first few stitches (Diagram 1). When the thread end is securely in place, clip the knot.

To stitch, push the needle up through a hole in the fabric, cross the thread intersection (or square) on a left-to-right diagonal (Diagram 2). Half the stitch is now completed.

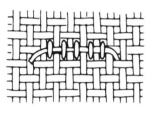

DIAGRAM 1
Reverse side of work

DIAGRAM 2

DIAGRAM 3

DIAGRAM 4

Next, cross back, right to left, forming an X (Diagram 3). Work all the same color stitches on one row, then cross back, completing the X's (Diagram 4).

Some needleworkers prefer to cross each stitch as they come to it. This method also works, but be sure all of the top stitches are slanted in the same direction. Isolated stitches must be crossed as they are worked. Vertical stitches are crossed as shown in Diagram 5.

At the top, work horizontal rows of a single color, left to right. This method allows you to go from an unoccupied space to an occupied space (working from an empty hole to a filled one), making ruffling of the floss less likely. Holes are used more than once, and all stitches "hold hands" unless a space is indicated on the chart. Hold the work upright throughout (do not turn as with many needlepoint stitches).

When carrying the thread from one area to another, run the needle under a few stitches on the wrong side. Do not carry thread across an open expanse of fabric as it will be visible from the front when the project is completed.

To end a color, weave in and out of the underside of the stitches, making a scallop stitch or two for extra security (Diagram 6).

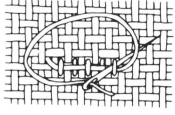

DIAGRAM 5

DIAGRAM 6
Reverse side of work

When possible, end in the same direction in which you were working, jumping up a row if necessary (Diagram 7). This prevents holes caused by stitches being pulled in two directions.

Trim the thread ends closely and do not leave any tails or knots as they will show through the fabric when the work is completed.

Backstitch (Diagram 8) is used for outlines, face details and the like. It is worked from hole to hole, and may be stitched as a vertical, horizontal or diagonal line.

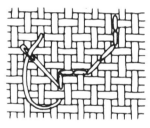

DIAGRAM 7
Reverse side of work

DIAGRAM 8

Embroidery on Linen. Working on linen requires a slightly different technique. While evenweave linen is remarkably regular, there are always a few thick or thin threads. To keep the stitches even, cross-stitch is worked over two threads in each direction (Diagram 9).

As you are working over more threads, linen affords a greater variation in stitches. A half-stitch can slant in either direction and is uncrossed. A three-quarters stitch is shown in Diagram 10.

Diagram 11 shows the backstitch worked on linen.

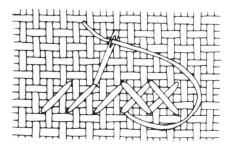

DIAGRAM 9

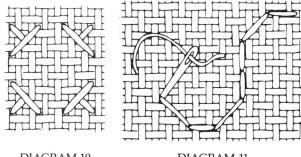

DIAGRAM 10   DIAGRAM 11

Embroidery on Gingham. Gingham and other checked fabrics can be used for cross-stitch. Using the fabric as a guide, work the stitches from corner to corner of each check.

Embroidery on Uneven-Weave Fabrics. If you wish to work cross-stitch on an uneven-weave fabric, baste a lightweight Penelope needlepoint canvas to the material. The design can then be stitched by working the cross-stitch over the double mesh of the canvas. When working in this manner, take care not to catch the threads of the canvas in the embroidery. After the cross-stitch is completed, remove the basting threads. With tweezers remove first the vertical threads, one strand at a time, of the needlepoint canvas, then the horizontal threads.

FINISHING

Wash the completed cross-stitch in cool water with mild soap. Rinse well, then roll in a towel to remove excess moisture (do not wring). Immediately iron on a well-padded surface, with embroidery right-side down. Allow the piece to dry completely before continuing.

Depending on your project, there are a number of ways to finish the cross-stitch. Tablecloths and place mats can be either hemmed or fringed. To mount a picture, center the work over a white, rag-content mat board. Turn the margins evenly to the back. Working first from top to bottom, lace the margins fairly tautly with sturdy thread. Next, continue to lace the work from side to side in the same manner. (Note: Never use glue for mounting cross-stitch.) Cotton and linen fabrics can be framed under glass; wool needs to breathe and should not be framed under glass unless a breathing space is left.

NEEDLEPOINT

One of the most common methods for working needlepoint is from a charted design. By simply viewing each square of a chart as a stitch on the canvas, the patterns quickly and easily translate from one technique to another.

MATERIALS

1. **Needles.** A blunt tapestry needle with a rounded tip and an elongated eye. The needle must clear the hole of the canvas without spreading the threads. For No. 10 canvas, a No. 18 needle works best.

2. **Canvas.** There are two distinct types of needlepoint canvas: single-mesh (mono canvas) and double-mesh (Penelope canvas). Single-mesh canvas, the more common of the two, is easier on the eyes as the spaces are slightly larger. Double-mesh canvas has two horizontal and two vertical threads forming each mesh. The latter is a very stable canvas on which the threads stay securely in place as the work progresses. Canvas is available in many

sizes, from 5 mesh-per-inch to 18 mesh-per-inch, and even smaller. The number of mesh-per-inch will, of course, determine the dimensions of the finished needlepoint project. A 60-square × 120-square chart will measure 12″ × 24″ on 5 mesh-to-the-inch canvas, 5″ × 10″ on 12 mesh-to-the-inch canvas. The most common canvas size is 10 to the inch.

3. **Yarns.** Persian, crewel and tapestry yarns all work well on needlepoint canvas.

PREPARING TO WORK

Allow 1″ to 1½″ blank canvas all around. Bind the raw edges of the canvas with masking tape or machine-stitched double-fold bias tape.

There are few hard-and-fast rules on where to begin the design. It is best to complete the main motif, then fill the background as the last step.

For any guidelines you wish to draw on the canvas, take care that your marking medium is waterproof. Nonsoluble inks, acrylic paints thinned with water so as not to clog the mesh, and waterproof felt-tip pens all work well. If unsure, experiment on a scrap of canvas.

When working with multiple strands (such as Persian yarn) always separate (strand) the yarn before beginning to stitch. This one small step allows for better coverage of the canvas. When you need more than one piece of yarn in the needle, use separate strands and do not double the yarn. For example: If you need two strands of 3-ply Persian yarn, use two separated strands. Yarn has a nap (just as fabrics do) and can be felt to be smoother in one direction than the other. Always work with the nap (the smooth side) pointing down.

For 5 mesh-to-the-inch canvas, use six strands of 3-ply yarn; for 10 mesh-to-the-inch canvas, use three strands of 3-ply yarn.

STITCHING

Cut yarn lengths 18″ long. Begin needlepoint by holding about 1″ of loose yarn on the wrong side of the work and working the first several stitches over the loose end to secure it. To end a piece of yarn, run it under several completed stitches on the wrong side of the work.

There are hundreds of needlepoint stitch variations, but tent stitch is universally considered to be *the* needlepoint stitch. The most familiar versions of tent stitch are half-cross stitch, continental stitch and basket-weave stitch.

Half-cross stitch *(Diagram 12)* is worked from left to right. The canvas is then turned around and the return row is again stitched from left to right. Holding the needle vertically, bring it to the front of the canvas through the hole that will be the bottom of the first stitch. Keep the stitches loose for minimum distortion and good coverage. Half-cross stitch is best worked on a double-mesh canvas.

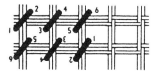

DIAGRAM 12

Continental stitch *(Diagram 13)* begins in the upper right-hand corner and is worked from right to left. The needle is slanted and always brought out a mesh ahead. The resulting stitch appears as a half-cross stitch on the front and as a slanting stitch on the back. When the row is complete, turn the canvas around to work the return row, continuing to stitch from right to left.

Basket-weave stitch *(Diagram 14)* begins in the upper right-hand corner with four continental stitches (two stitches worked horizontally across the top and two placed directly below the first stitch). Work diagonal rows, the first slanting up and across the canvas from right to left, and the next down and across from left to right. Moving down the canvas from left to right, the

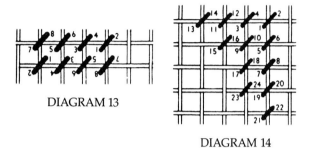

DIAGRAM 13

DIAGRAM 14

needle is in a vertical position; working in the opposite direction, the needle is horizontal. The rows interlock, creating a basket-weave pattern on the wrong side. If the stitch is not done properly, a faint ridge will show where the pattern was interrupted. On basket-weave stitch, always stop working in the middle of a row, rather than at the end, so that you will know in which direction you were working.

FINISHING

When the needlepoint is complete, it must be blocked to give it a professional look. Any hard, flat surface you do not mind marring with nail holes, and that will not warp with dampness, can serve as a blocking board. A piece of plywood, an old drawing board, an old-fashioned doily blocker will all work well.

Moisten a terry-cloth towel in cold water and roll the needlepoint in the towel. Leave the needlepoint in the towel overnight to insure that both the canvas and yarn are thoroughly and evenly dampened. Do not saturate the canvas and never hold it under the faucet as that much water is not necessary.

Mark the desired finished size of the needlepoint on the blocking board, taking care that all corners are straight. Stretch the finished canvas on the board, right-side down, and tack the margins with thumbtacks spaced about ½" apart. It may take some pulling to get the needlepoint straight, but do not be afraid of this stress. Leave the canvas on the blocking board, away from direct sun and heat, until thoroughly dry. (Note: Never place an iron on the needlepoint; you cannot successfully block with a steam iron as the canvas must dry in the straightened position.)

KNITTING

Charted designs can be worked into stockinette stitch as you are knitting, or they can be embroidered with duplicate stitch when the knitting is complete. For the former, wind the different colors of yarn on bobbins and work in the same manner as in Fair Isle knitting. A few quick Fair Isle tips: (1) Always bring up the new color yarn from under the dropped color to prevent holes. (2) Carry the color not in use loosely across the wrong side of the work, but not more than three or four stitches without twisting the yarns. If a color is not in use for more than seven or eight stitches, it is usually best to drop that color yarn and rejoin a new bobbin when the color is again needed.

CROCHETING

There are a number of ways in which charts can be used for crochet. Among them are:

SINGLE CROCHET

Single crochet is often seen worked in multiple colors. When changing colors, always pick up the new color for the last yarn-over of the old color. The color not in use can be carried loosely across the back of the work for a few stitches, or you can work the single crochet over the unused color. The latter method makes for a neater appearance on the wrong side, but sometimes the old color peeks through the stitches. This method can also be applied to half-double crochet and double crochet, but keep in mind that the longer stitches will distort the design.

FILET CROCHET

This technique is nearly always worked from charts and uses only one color thread. The result is a solid-color piece with the design filled in and the background left as an open mesh. Care must be taken in selecting the design, as the longer stitch causes distortion.

AFGHAN CROCHET

The most common method here is cross-stitch worked over the afghan stitch. Complete the afghan crochet project. Then, following the chart for color placement, work cross-stitch over the squares of crochet.

OTHER CHARTED METHODS

Latch hook, Assisi embroidery, beading, cross-stitch on needlepoint canvas (a European favorite) and lace net embroidery are among the other needlework methods worked from charts.

SIX STRAND EMBROIDERY COTTON (FLOSS) CONVERSION CHART

KEY: T = Possible Substitute   * = Close Match   — = No Match

DMC NO.	ROYAL MOULINÉ NO.	BATES/ANCHOR NO.
White	1001	2
Ecru	8600	926
208	3335*	110*
209	3415*	105
210	3320*	104
211	3410	108*
221	2570	897*
223	2555	894
224	2545	893
225	2540	892
300	8330	352*
301	8315*	349*
304	2415*	47*
307	6005*	289*
309	2525*	42*
310	1002	403
311	4275T	149*
312		147*
315	3130	896*
316	3120	895*
317	1030*	400*
318	1020*	399*
319	5025	246*
320	5015	216*
321	2415	47
322		978*
326	2530*	59*
327	3365*	101*
333		119
334	4250T	145
335	2525T	42*
336	4270*	149*
340		118
341		117
347	2425*	13*
349	2400	13
350	2045T	11
351	2015T	11*
352	2015	10*
353	2010*	8*
355	8095	5968
356	8090	5975*
367	5020	216*
368	5005*	240*
369	5005	213*
370		889*
371		888*
372		887*
400	8325*	351
402	8305*	347*
407	8005*	882*
413	1025*	401
414	1020*	400*
415	1015	398
420	8720*	375*
422	8710*	373*
433	8265	371*
434	8215	309
435	8210*	369*
436	8205	363*

DMC NO.	ROYAL MOULINÉ NO.	BATES/ANCHOR NO.
437	8200*	362
444	6155*	291
445	6000	288
451		399*
452		399*
453		397*
469	1015T	267*
470	5255*	267
471	5245	266*
472	5240	264*
498	2425T	20*
500	5125	879*
501	5120*	878
502	5110	876
503	5105	875
504	5100	213*
517	4860*	169*
518	4855T	168*
519		167*
520		862*
522		859*
523		859*
524	1115T	858*
535		401*
543	8500	933*
550	3380*	102*
552	3370*	101
553	3360	98
554	3355*	96*
561		212*
562		210*
563		208*
564		203*
580	5935	267*
581	5925	266*
597	4860*	168*
598	4855*	167*
600	2225*	59*
601	2225*	78*
602	2640*	77*
603	2720*	76*
604	2710	75*
605	2155	50*
606	7260	335
608	7255	333*
610	5825T	889*
611	5735T	898
612	8815*	832
613	5605*	956*
632	8530	936*
640	8625	903
642	8620*	392
644	8800	830
645	1115	905*
646	1115*	8581
647	1110	8581*
648	1100*	900
666	2405	46
676	6250	891
677		886*

DMC NO.	ROYAL MOULINÉ NO.	BATES/ANCHOR NO.
680	6260*	901
699	5375	923*
700	5365*	229
701	5365*	227
702	5330	239
703	5320	238
704	5310*	256*
712	8600*	387*
718	3015*	88
720	—	326
721	—	324*
722	—	323*
725	6215	306*
726	6150*	295
727	6135	293
729	6255	890
730	—	924*
731	—	281*
732	5925T	281*
733	—	280*
734	—	279*
738	8245*	942
739	8240*	885*
740	7045	316
741	6125	304
742	6120	303
743	6210	297
744	6110*	301*
745	6105	300*
746	6100	386*
747	4850	158*
754	8075	778*
758	8080	868
760	2035	9*
761	2030	8*
762	1010*	397
772	—	264*
775	4600*	128*
776	2110	24*
778	3110	968*
780	8215*	310*
781	8215	309*
782	6230	308
783	6220*	307
791	4165*	941*
792	4155T	940
793	4155	121
794	4145	120*
796	4340	133*
797	4265*	132*
798	4325	131*
799	4310*	130*
800	4310	128
801	8405	357*
806	4870T	169*
807	4860*	168*
809	4145*	130*
813	4610*	160*
814	2340T	44*
815	2530*	43

DMC NO.	ROYAL MOULINÉ NO.	BATES/ANCHOR NO.
816	2530	44*
817	2415T	19
818	2505*	48
819	2000	892*
820	4345	134
822	8605*	387*
823	4400*	150
824	4225	164*
825	4215	162*
826	4210	161*
827	4605	159*
828	4850	158*
829	5825	906
830	5825*	889*
831	5825T	889*
832	5815	907
833	5815*	874*
834	5810*	874
838	8425*	380*
839	8560	380*
840	8555	379*
841	8550	378*
842	8505	376*
844	1115T	401*
869	8720*	944*
890	5025*	879*
891	2135	35*
892	2130	28
893	2125*	27
894	2115T	26
895	5430*	246*
898	8425*	360
899	2515	27*
900	7230*	333
902	—	72*
904	5295*	258*
905	5295	258*
906	5285*	256*
907	5280*	255
909	5370	229*
910	5370*	228*
911	5465*	205*
912	5465	205
913	5460*	209
915	3030	89*
917	3020*	89*
918	8330*	341*
919	8095*	341*
920	8060*	339*
921	8060T	349*
922	8315T	324*
924	4830T	851*
926	4820*	779*
927	4810T	849*
928	1010T	900*
930	4510	922*
931	4505	921*
932	4500	920*
934	5070T	862*
935	5225T	862*

DMC NO.	ROYAL MOULINÉ NO.	BATES/ANCHOR NO.
936	5260T	269
937	5260	268
938	8430	381
939	4405	127
943	4935*	188*
945	8020*	347*
946	7230*	332*
947	7255*	330*
948	8070	778*
950	8020T	4146
951	8020T	366*
954	5455*	203*
955	5450	206*
956	2170*	40*
957	2160T	40*
958	—	187
959	—	186
961	2515*	76*
962	2515	76*
963	2505	49*
964	—	185
966	5150*	214*
970	7040	316*
971	7045	316*
972	6120*	298
973	6015	290
975	8365	355*
976	8355	308*
977	8350	307*
986	5430	246*
987	5020T	244*
988	5295T	243*
989	5405T	242*
991	5165T	189*
992	4925T	187*
993	4915*	186*
995	4710	410
996	4700	433
3011	5525T	845*
3012	5525*	844*
3013	5515	842*
3021	—	382*
3022	—	8581*
3023	—	8581*
3024	1100	900*
3031	—	905*
3032	8620T	903*
3033	8610*	388*
3041	3215*	871
3042	3205*	869
3045	6260T	373*
3046	5810	887*
3047	5805	886*
3051	5530T	846*
3052	5060*	859*
3053	5055*	859*
3064	8005*	914*
3072	4805*	397*
3078	6130	292*
3325	4200	159*

DMC NO.	ROYAL MOULINÉ NO.	BATES/ANCHOR NO.
3326	2115*	25*
3328	2045	11*
3340	—	329
3341	—	328
3345	5025T	268*
3346	5220T	257*
3347	5210*	266*
3348	5270*	265
3350	2220	42*
3354	2210	74*
3362	—	862*
3363	—	861*
3364	8435	843*
3371	—	382
3607	—	87*
3608	—	86
3609	—	85
3685	2335	70*
3687	2325	69*
3688	2320	66*
3689	2310	49
3705	—	35*
3706	—	28*
3708	—	26*
48	9000*	1201*
51	9014	1220
52	9006	1208
53	—	
57	9002	1203
61	9013T	1218*
62	9000T	1201*
67	—	1211*
69	—	1218*
75	9002	1206*
90	9012T	1217
91	9008*	1211
92	9011T	1216*
93	9007*	1210*
94	9011*	1216
95	9006T	1208*
99	9005T	1207*
101	9009*	1213*
102	—	1208*
103	—	1210*
104	9012	1217
105	9013*	1218
106	9002T	1203*
107	9003	1204
108	9014*	1220*
111	9007*	1218*
112	9003T	1204*
113	9007*	1210*
114	9010	1215
115	9004	1206
121	9007	1210
122	9010T	1215*
123	—	1213*
124	9007T	1210*
125	9009	1213
126	9006*	1208*

Reproduced by permission of the copyright owner, The American School of Needlework, Inc.

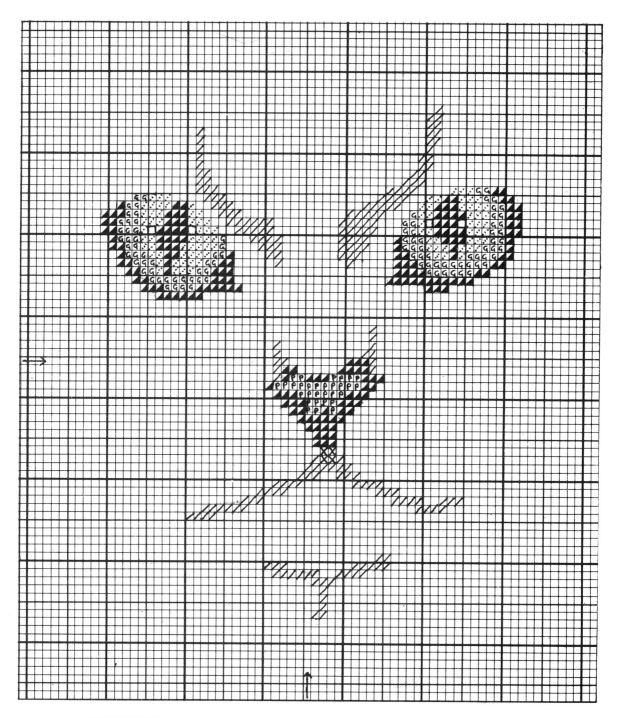

DUCHESS

(See color illustration on inside front cover.)

DMC #

◪	310	Black
⊠	318	Light Steel Gray
◪	762	Very Light Pearl Gray
◙	772	Very Light Loden Green
℗	963	Very Light Dusty Rose
⊡	966	Medium Baby Green
☐		*Snow White for background

*For cross-stitch, use white fabric and leave the background stitches unworked.

C IS FOR CAT ▶

DMC #

◼	310	Black
⊠	452	Medium Shell Gray
◎	453	Light Shell Gray
◙	772	Very Light Loden Green
℗	818	Baby Pink
⊡	3072	Very Light Beaver Gray
◪	3348	Light Yellow Green

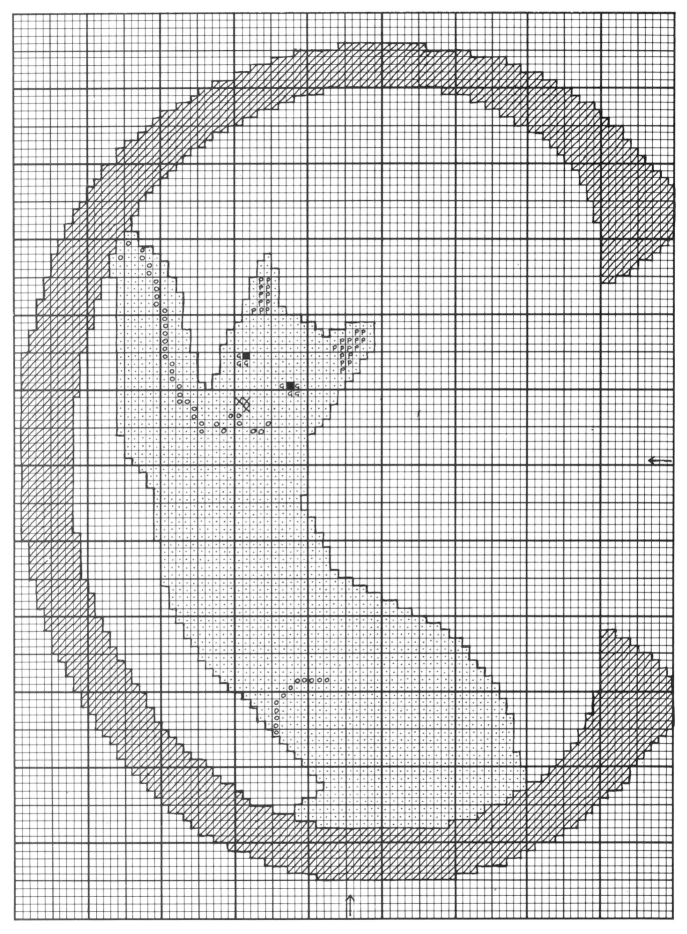

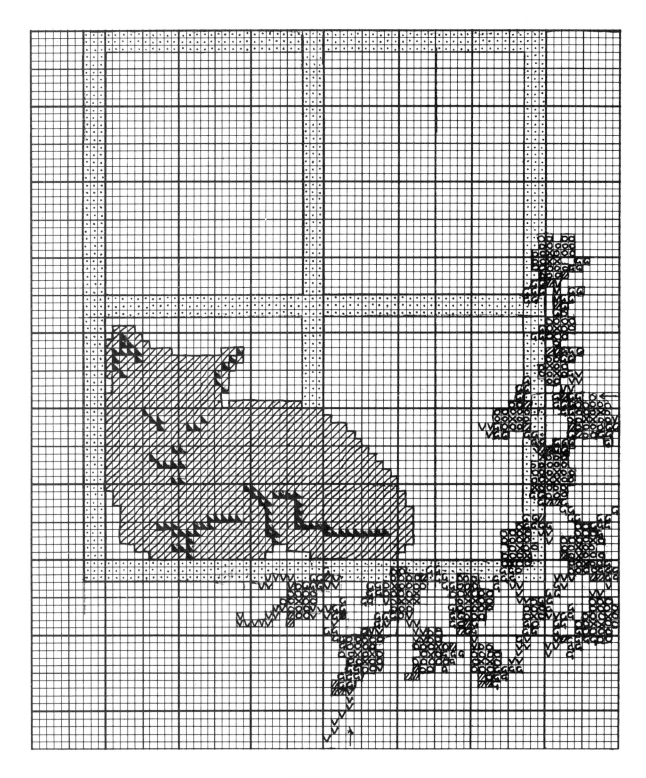

LAZY SUMMER DAYS

(See color illustration on back cover.)

DMC #

	310	Black to fill inside of window	▨	699	Christmas Green
⒢	320	Medium Pistachio Green	▨	738	Very Light Tan
◣	436	Tan	⃝	963	Very Light Dusty Rose
Ⅵ	504	Light Blue Green	☐	3078	*Very Light Golden Yellow for background
☒	605	Very Light Cranberry	·		Snow White

*For cross-stitch, use pale yellow fabric and leave the background stitches unworked.

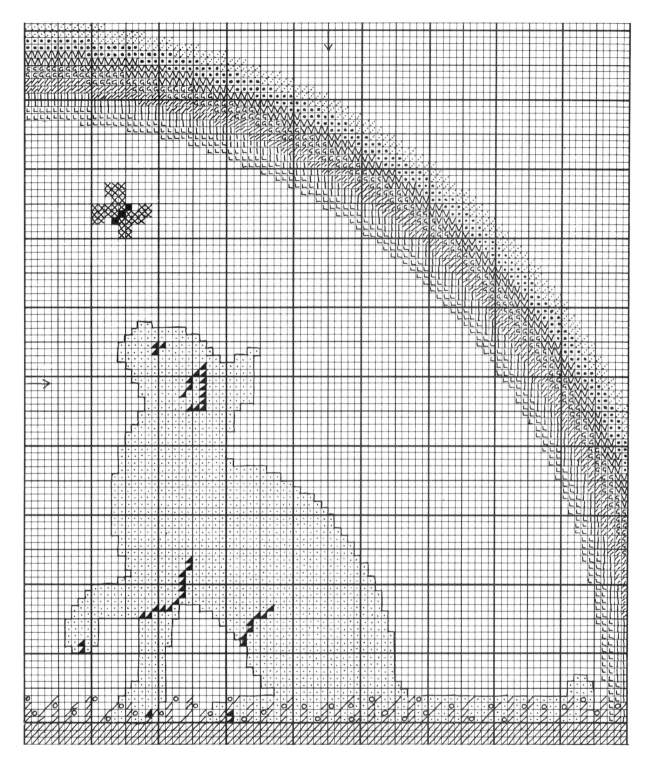

CURIOSITY

DMC #

L	210	Medium Lavender
■	310	Black
◿	368	Light Pistachio Green
◉	726	Light Topaz
◢	762	Very Light Pearl Gray

G	772	Very Light Loden Green
I	775	Light Baby Blue
◿	799	Medium Delft Blue
□	800	*Pale Delft Blue for Background
◉	945	Light Apricot

∴	963	Very Light Dusty Rose
⊠	996	Medium Electric Blue
V	3078	Very Light Golden Yellow
·		Snow White

*For cross-stitch, use light blue fabric and leave the background stitches unworked.

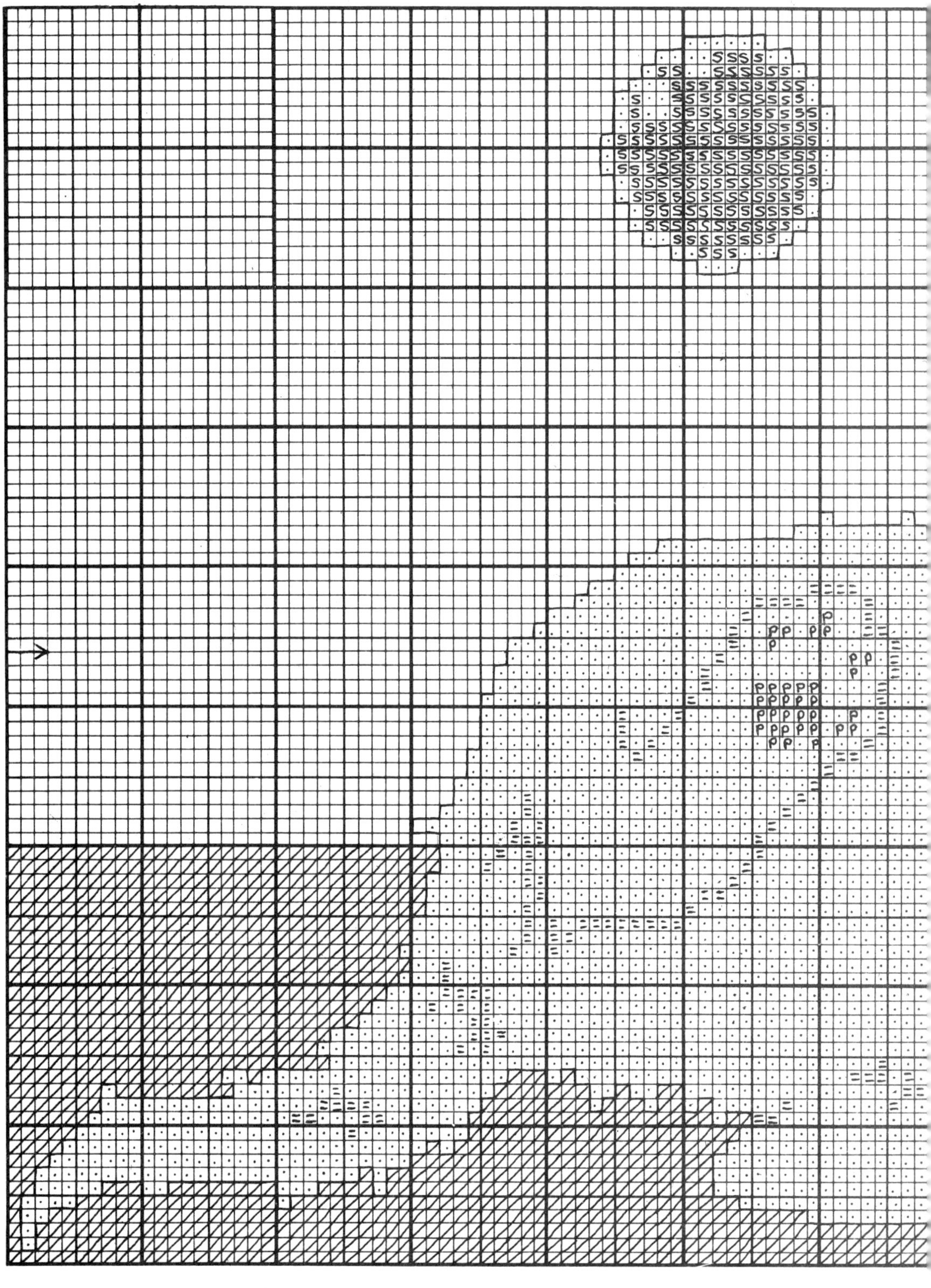

BUBBLES

(See color illustration on inside front cover.)

DMC #

◢	310	Black		S	775	Light Baby Blue
⊟	453	Light Shell Gray		O	799	Medium Delft Blue
◿	602	Medium Cranberry		P	963	Very Light Dusty Rose
☐	604	*Light Cranberry for background		·		Snow White

*For cross-stitch, use light cranberry fabric and leave the background stitches unworked.

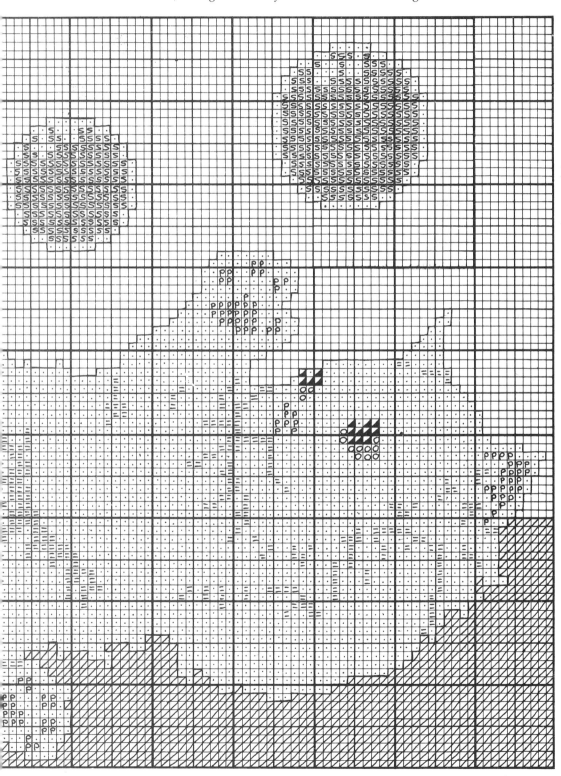

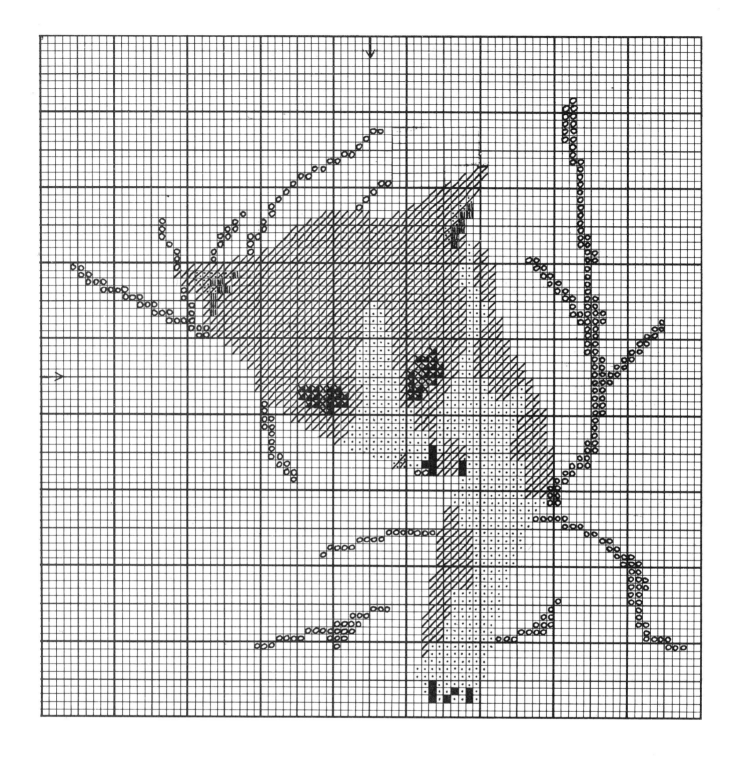

SLEEP TIGHT

DMC #

⊠	310	Black	▨	819	Light Baby Pink	◪	966	Medium Baby Green
▧	762	Very Light Pearl Gray	⊙	957	Pale Geranium Pink	·		Snow White
▥	818	Baby Pink	☐	963	*Very Light Dusty Rose for background	■		Ecru

*For cross-stitch, use light rose fabric and leave the background stitches unworked.

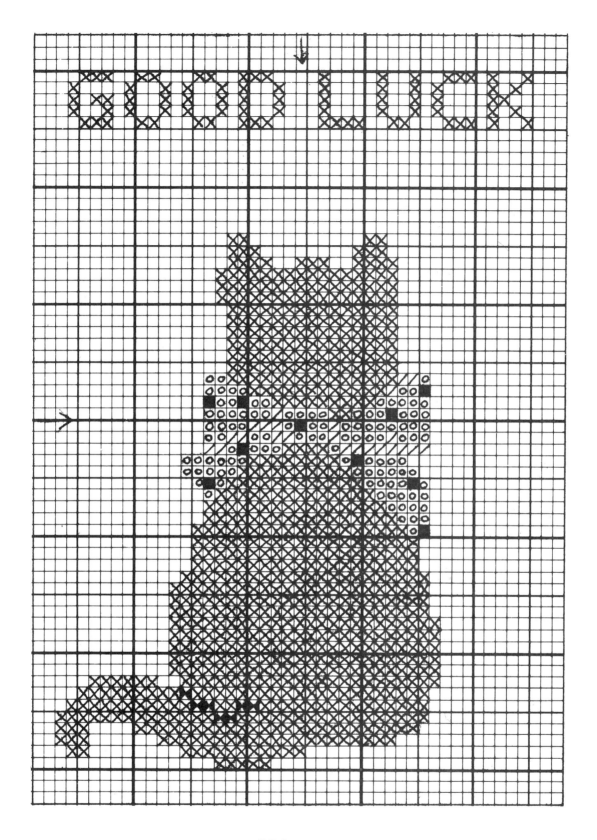

GOOD LUCK

(See color illustration on back cover.)

DMC #

☒	310	Black	■	762	Very Light Pearl Gray
⊡	321	Christmas Red	⧄	814	Dark Garnet Red
⊠	415	Pearl Gray			

REDPOINT SIAMESE

DMC #

■	310	Black	B	820	Very Dark Royal Blue
Ⅲ	402	Very Light Mahogany	O	945	Light Apricot
·	797	Royal Blue	◪	951	Very Light Apricot
☐	800	*Pale Delft Blue for background	P	963	Very Light Dusty Rose
⊠	809	Delft Blue	⁄		Ecru

*For cross-stitch, use pale blue fabric and leave the background stitches unworked.

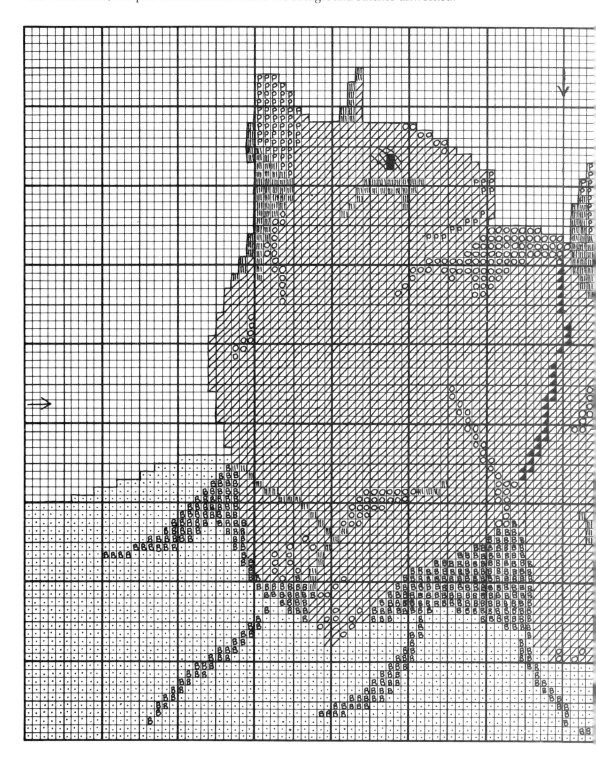

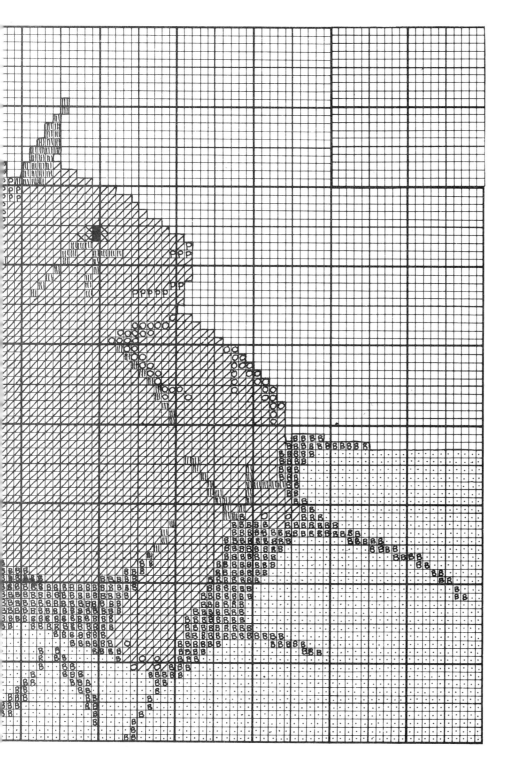

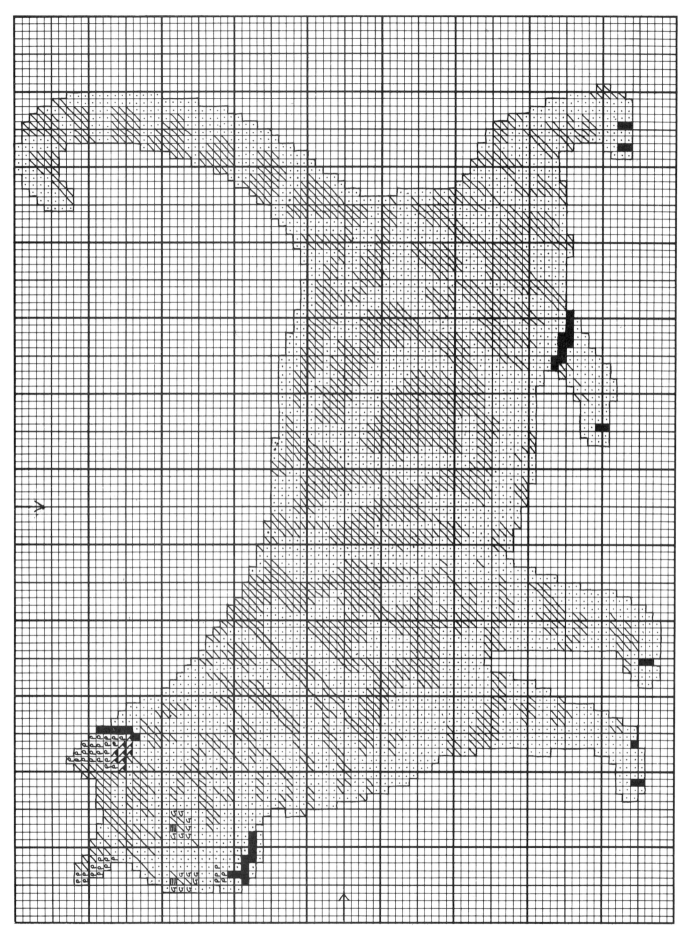

▲ TABBY

DMC #

☑	310	Black
■	452	Medium Shell Gray
·	453	Light Shell Gray
◢	772	Very Light Loden Green

◣	776	Medium Pink
P	818	Baby Pink
▤		Snow White

KITTEN AT PLAY ▼

DMC #

■	310	Black
C	333	Dark Lilac
□	341	*Light Lilac for background
◢	666	Bright Christmas Red

☑	762	Very Light Pearl Gray
Ⓑ	800	Pale Delft Blue
P	818	Baby Pink
·		Snow White

*For cross-stitch, use lilac fabric and leave the background stitches unworked.

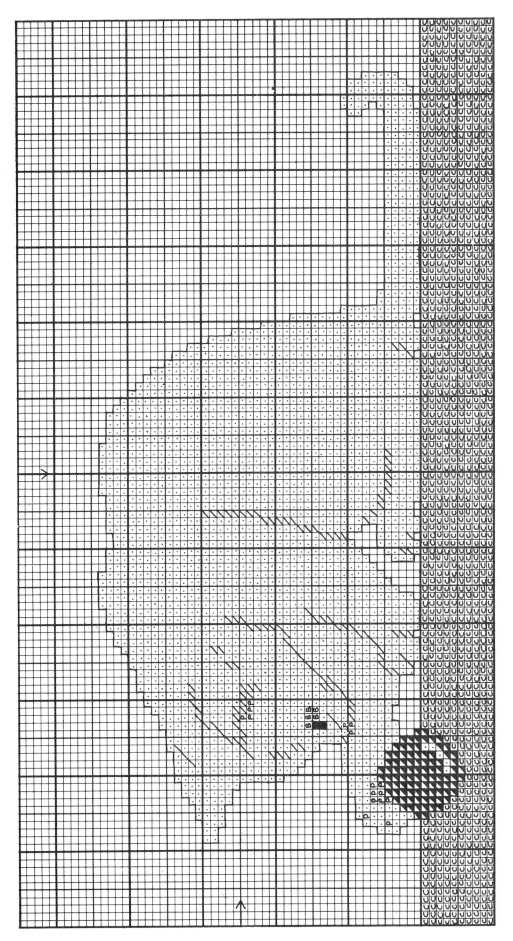

19

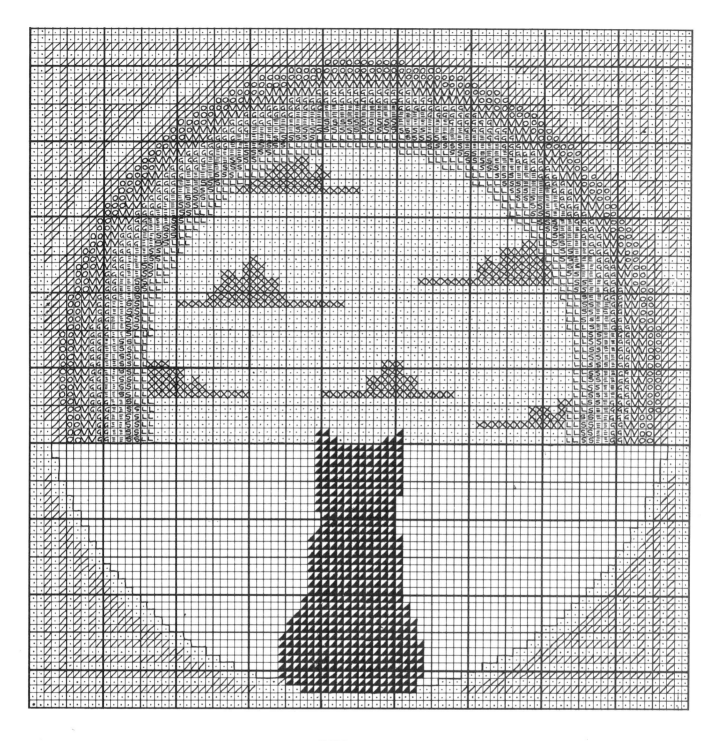

OLD TIMER

DMC

Ⓛ	210	Medium Lavender	·	800	Pale Delft Blue	☐	955	*Light Nile Green for
◢	310	Black	☰	809	Delft Blue			background
Ⓠ	772	Very Light Loden Green	Ⓞ	945	Light Apricot	⊻	3078	Very Light Golden Yellow
Ⓢ	775	Light Baby Blue	⧄	963	Very Light Dusty Rose	⊠		Snow White

*For cross-stitch, use light green fabric and leave the background stitches unworked.

GOING HOME

DMC #

B	310	Black	□	704	*Bright Chartreuse for background
■	318	Light Steel Gray	S	762	Very Light Pearl Gray
⊠	321	Christmas Red	·	800	Pale Delft Blue
⊟	435	Very Light Brown	◪	3072	Very Light Beaver Gray
o	702	Kelly Green	⁄		Snow White

*For cross-stitch, use chartreuse fabric and leave the background stitches unworked.

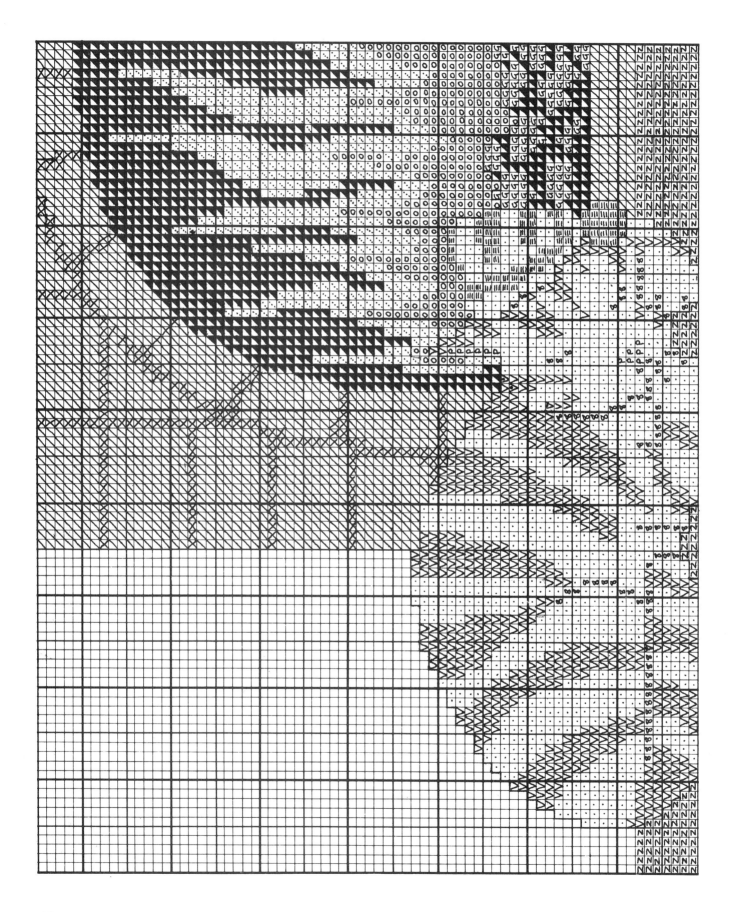

▲ FIRESIDE COMPANION

DMC #

☒	301	Medium Mahogany Brown			◐	970	Light Pumpkin
◣	310	Black			∴	973	Bright Canary Yellow
◪	644	Medium Beige Gray			☑	977	Light Golden Brown
☐	739	*Fawn Beige for background			☒	3072	Very Light Beaver Gray
◲	762	Very Light Pearl Gray			⊡		Snow White
▥	800	Pale Delft Blue			◙		Ecru
℗	818	Baby Pink					

*For cross-stitch, use light beige fabric and leave the background stitches unworked.

MOTHER'S PRIDE AND JOY ▼

DMC #

◹	210	Medium Lavender			ℙ	818	Baby Pink
◮	318	Light Steel Gray			◉	977	Light Golden Brown
◩	712	Cream			☐		*Snow White for background
◉	762	Very Light Pearl Gray			∶		Ecru
☑	772	Very Light Loden Green					

Outline the kittens in backstitch—762 Very Light Pearl Gray for the kitten on the left and 977 Light Golden Brown for the kitten on the right.

*For cross-stitch, use white fabric and leave the background stitches unworked.

23

GARDEN GAMES

(See color illustration on inside front cover.)

Symbol	DMC #	Color
▨	310	Black
◪	415	Pearl Gray
W	472	Very Pale Avocado Green
■	726	Light Topaz
·	762	Very Light Pearl Gray
☒	772	Very Light Loden Green
⁘	799	Medium Delft Blue
□	800	*Pale Delft Blue for background
O	945	Light Apricot
◿	963	Very Light Dusty Rose
G	966	Medium Baby Green
V	3078	Very Light Golden Yellow
L	3608	Fuchsia
B	3609	Light Fuchsia
⁄		Snow White

*For cross-stitch, use pale blue fabric and leave the background stitches unworked.

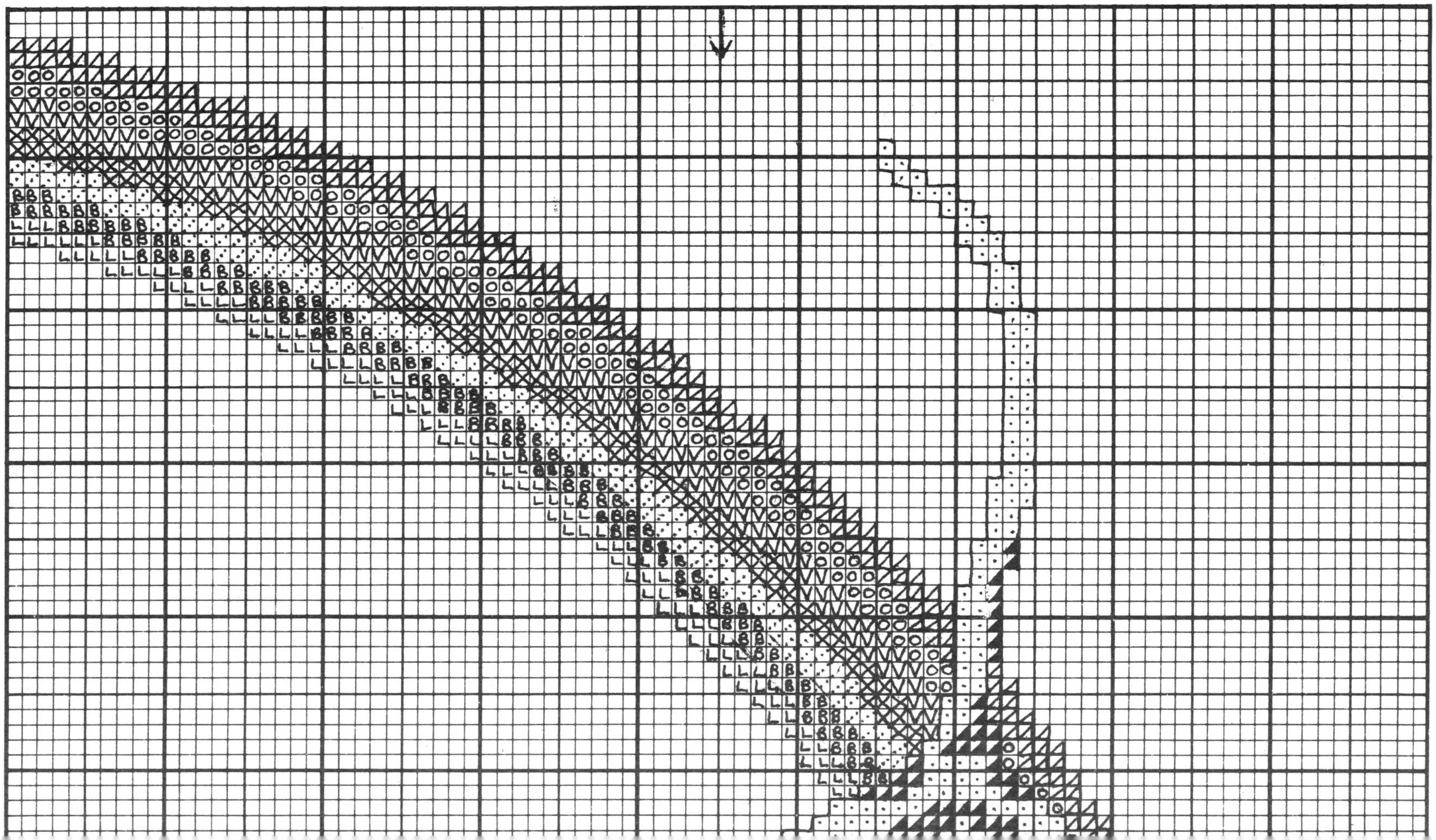

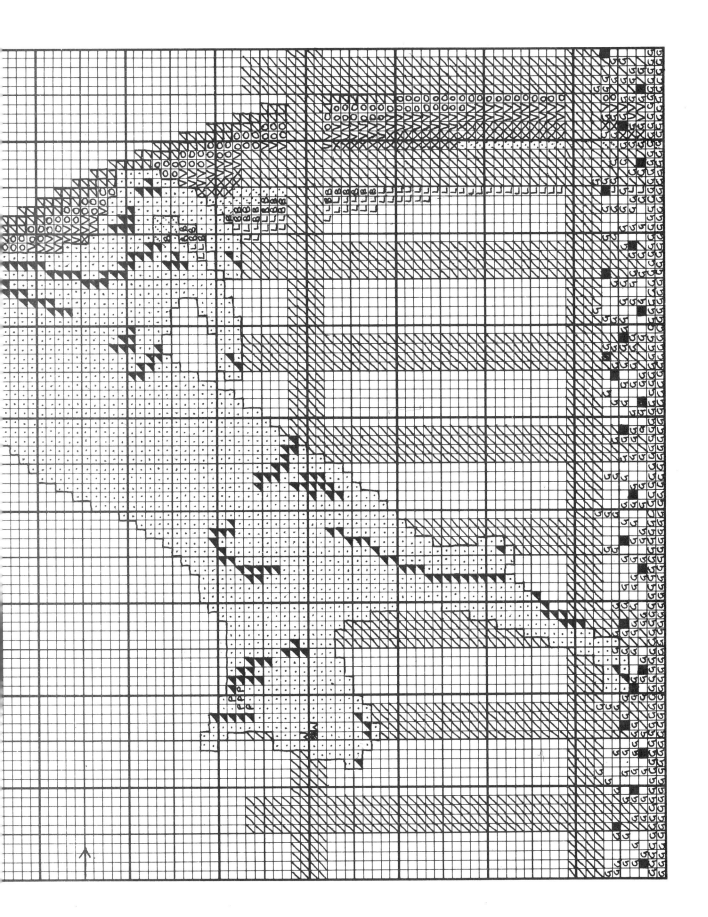

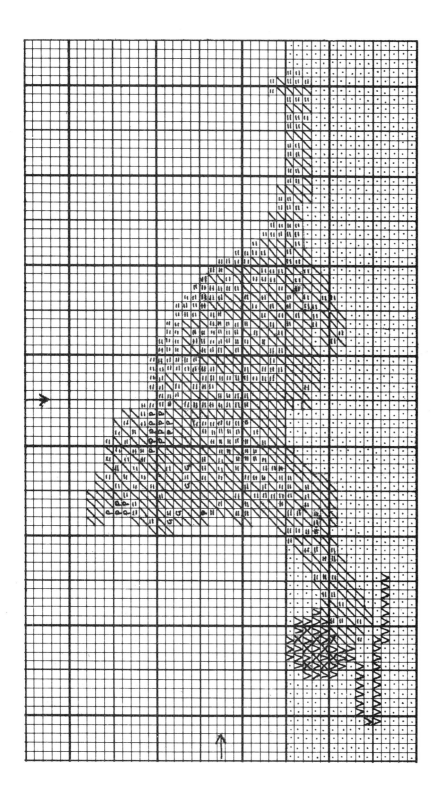

KITTEN WITH MILK JUG ▼

DMC #

◣	310	Black	◪	796	Dark Royal Blue
◧	415	Pearl Gray	⠒	798	Dark Delft Blue
◺	712	Cream	▦	809	Delft Blue
◎	746	Off White	P	818	Baby Pink
◿	762	Very Light Pearl Gray	☐	828	*Very Pale Blue for background
✕	772	Very Light Loden Green	•		Snow White

*For cross-stitch, use pale blue fabric and leave the background stitches unworked.

◀ KITTEN WITH WOOL

DMC #

▥	310	Black
◿	453	Light Shell Gray
◺	666	Bright Christmas Red
☐	775	*Light Baby Blue for background
✕	816	Garnet Red
P	818	Baby Pink
•	3078	Very Light Golden Yellow

*For cross-stitch, use light blue fabric and leave the background stitches unworked.

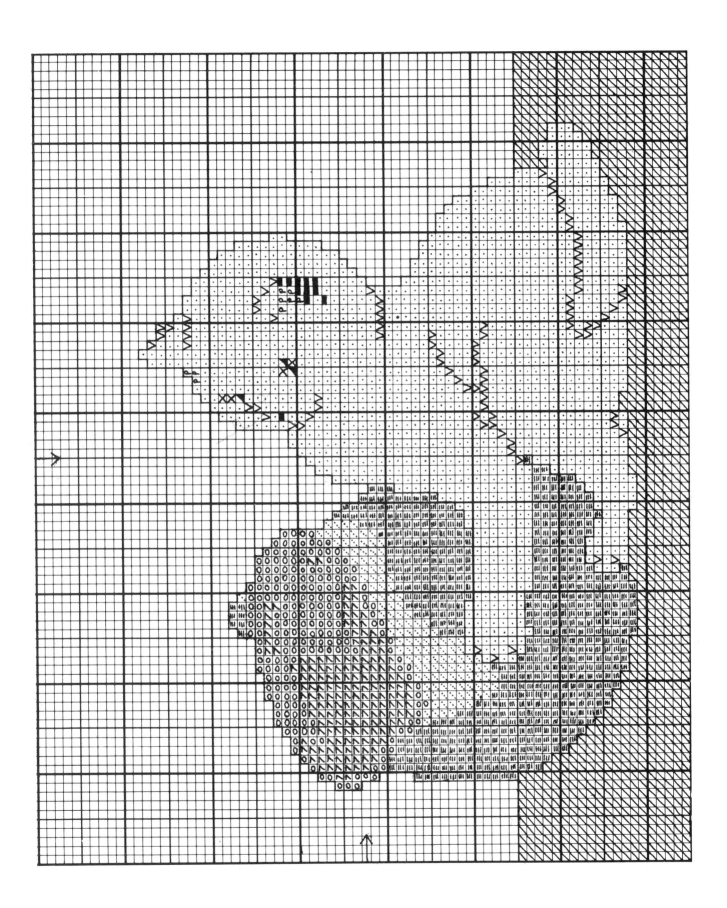

GARDEN SWING

DMC #

◼	310	Black	▨	677	Very Light Old Gold	
◤	367	Dark Pistachio Green	☒	725	Topaz	
꒖	368	Light Pistachio Green	▥	762	Very Light Pearl Gray	
▽	435	Very Light Brown	◼	776	Medium Pink	
꒒	519	Sky Blue	☐	800	*Pale Delft Blue for background	
			P	818	Baby Pink	
			N	3023	Light Brown Gray	
			S	3024	Very Light Brown Gray	
			O	3072	Very Light Beaver Gray	
			·		Snow White	

*For cross-stitch, use pale blue fabric and leave the background stitches unworked.

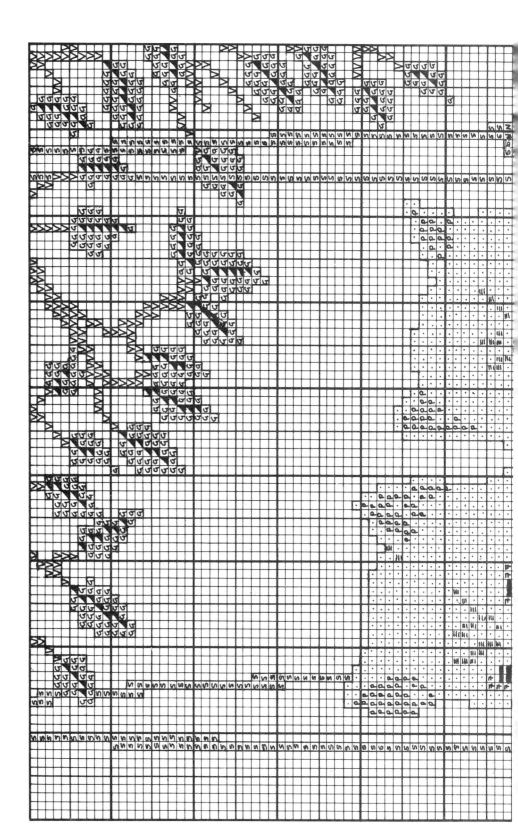

28

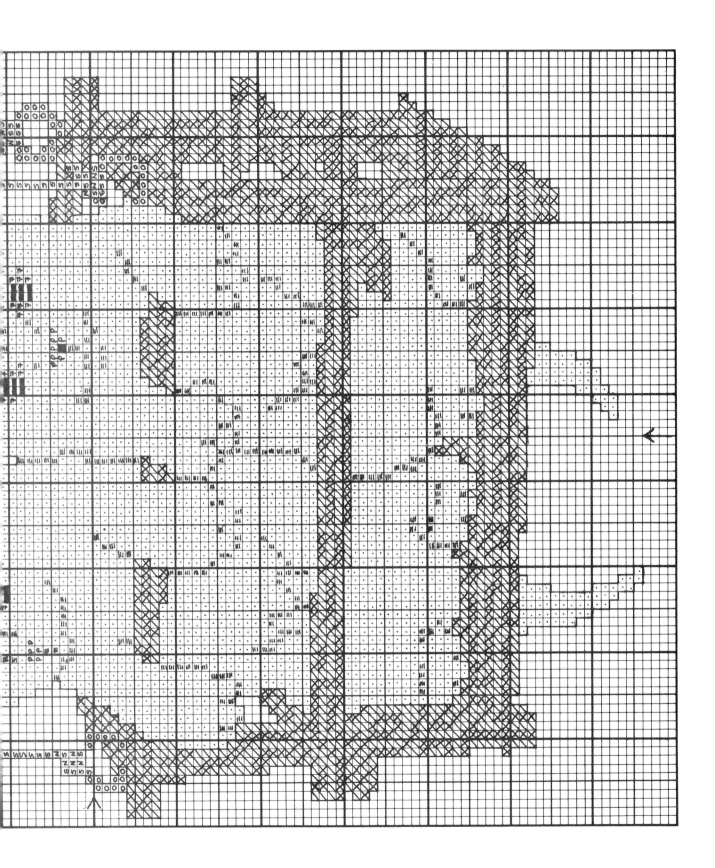

SUNSET SILHOUETTE

DMC #

⊡	310	Black		⊙	971	Pumpkin
☐	444	*Dark Lemon Yellow for background		⊿	972	Yellow Orange

*For cross-stitch, use bright yellow fabric and leave the background stitches unworked.

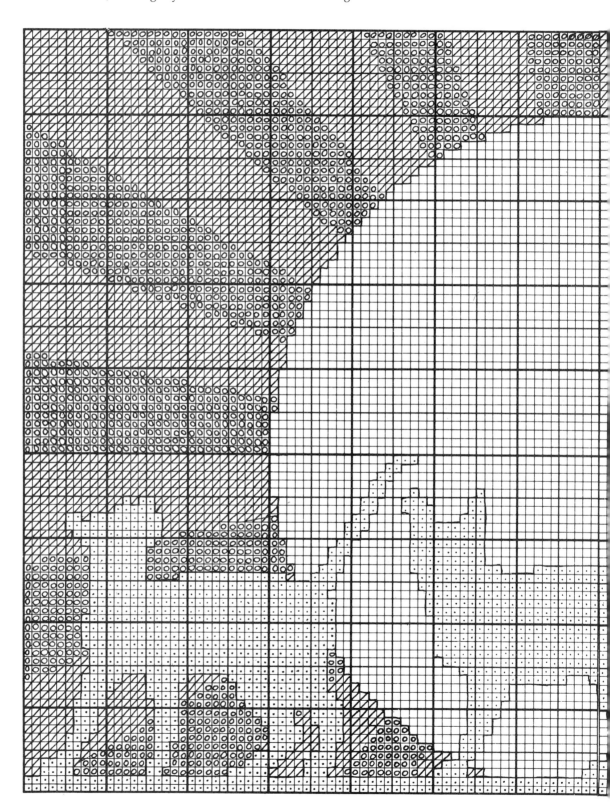

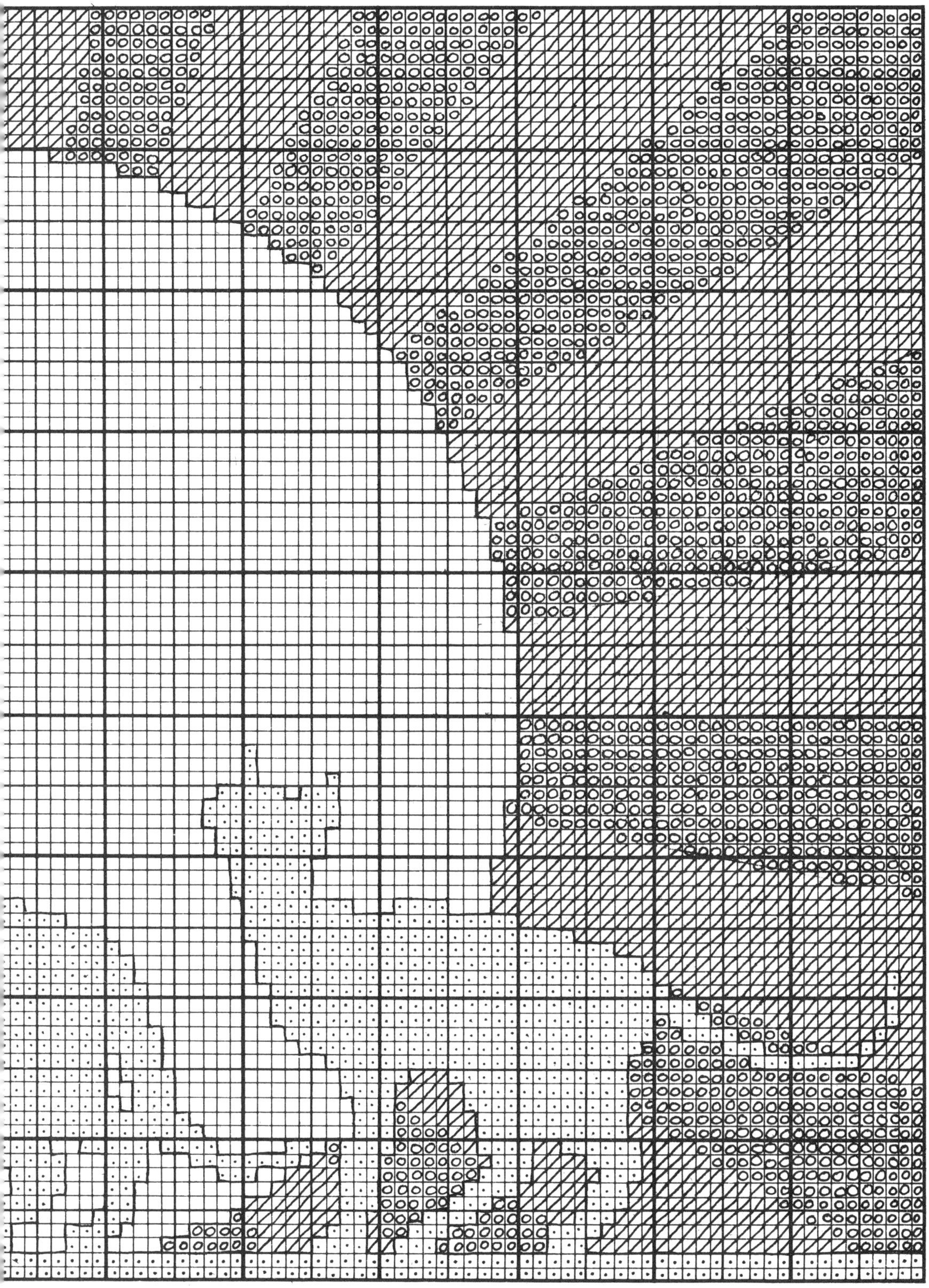

CATS BY MOONLIGHT

DMC #

☐   312   *Light Navy Blue for background   ⊡   Snow White for moon

⬲   3325   Baby Blue   ■   Snow White for stars

*For cross-stitch, use navy fabric and leave the background stitches unworked.

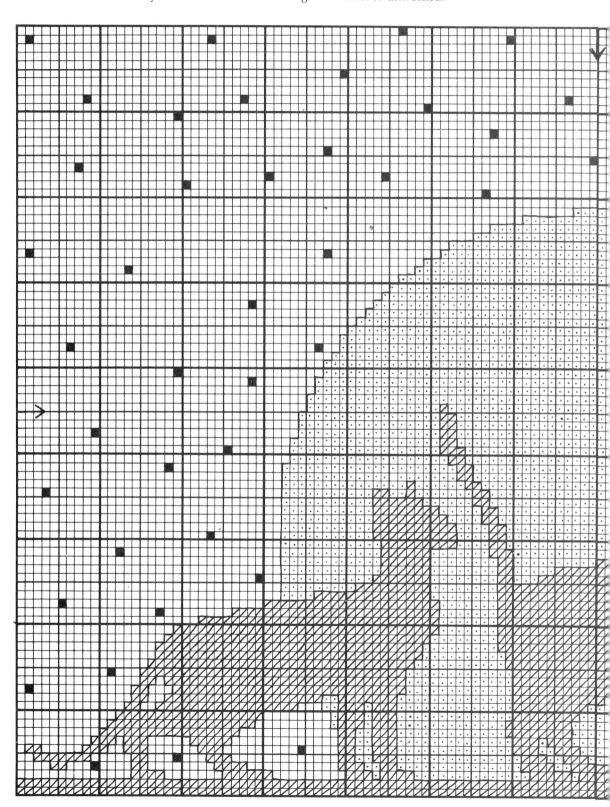

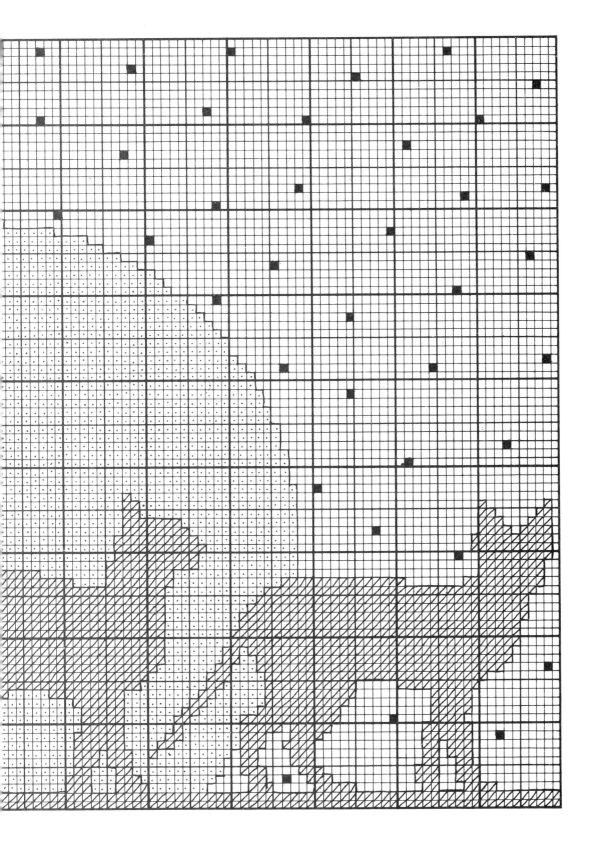

OVER THE RAINBOW

(See color illustration on inside front cover.)

DMC #

⊙	211	Light Lavender		☑	3078	Very Light Golden Yellow
⊠	772	Very Light Loden Green		☐	3325	*Baby Blue for background
⊡	809	Delft Blue		⧄	3609	Light Fuchsia
⊟	945	Light Apricot		·		Snow White
△	963	Very Light Dusty Rose				

*For cross-stitch, use baby blue fabric and leave the background stitches unworked.

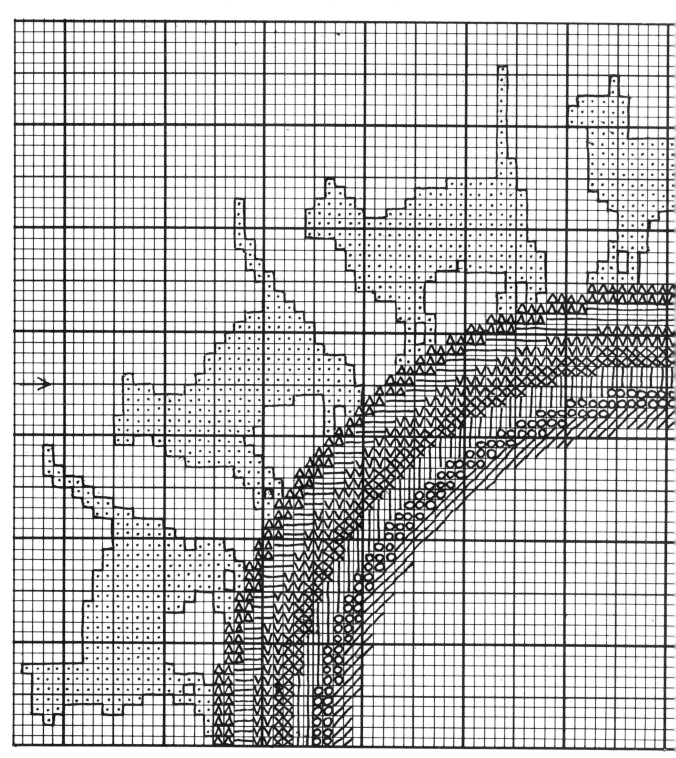

34

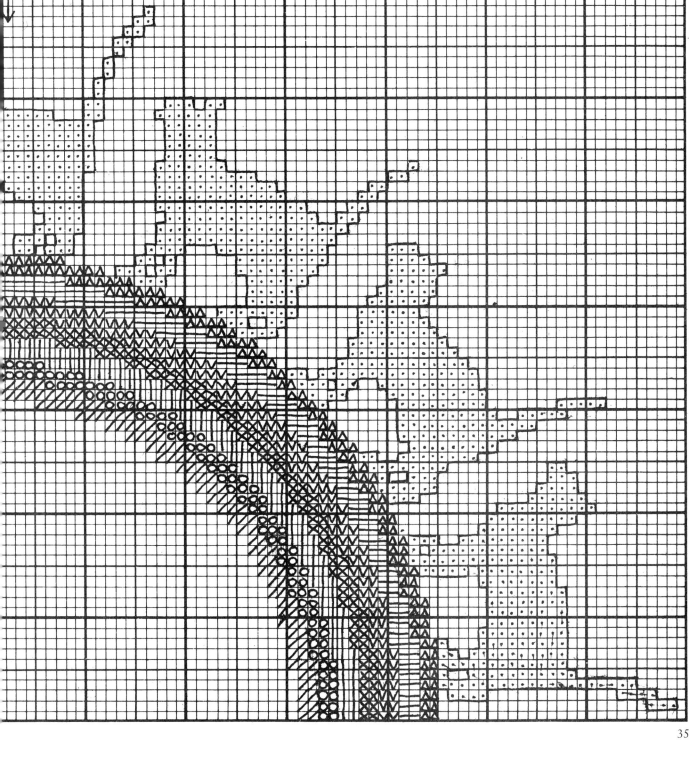

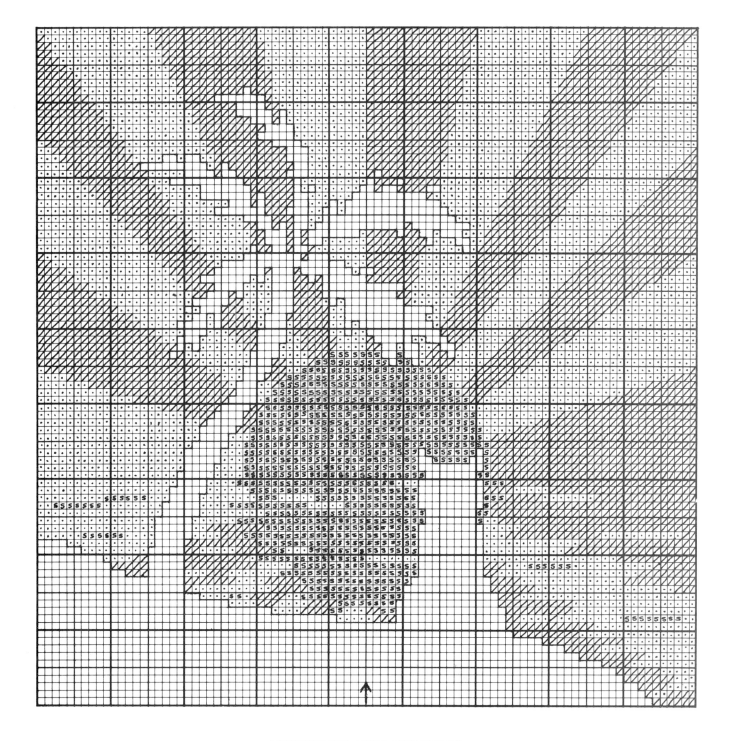

DESERT ISLAND DELIGHT

(See color illustration on inside back cover.)

DMC #

☐ 310 Black
⊡ 742 *Light Tangerine for background
⊘ 970 Light Pumpkin
Ⓢ 973 Bright Canary Yellow

*For cross-stitch, use light tangerine fabric and leave
the boxes indicated by ⊡ on the chart unworked.

CIRCULAR CAT MEDALLION
(See color illustration on inside back cover.)

Work the cat in 321 Christmas Red and the remainder
of the pattern in 57 Shaded Reds.

CAT BANNER

DMC #

⊡ 123   Shaded Aquas

☒ 958   Dark Aqua

Or, use colors desired.

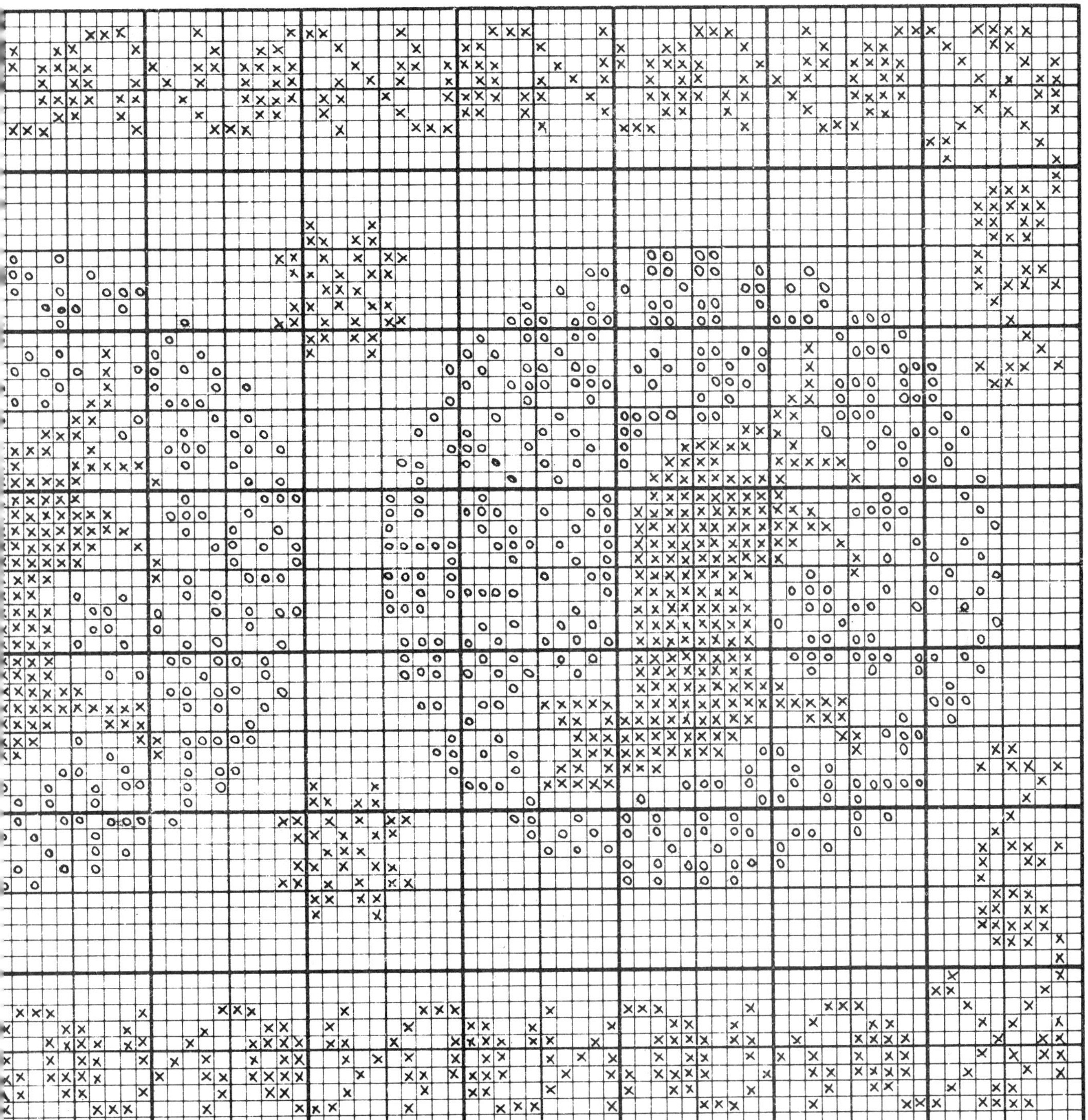

FILIGREE SQUARE

Use color desired.

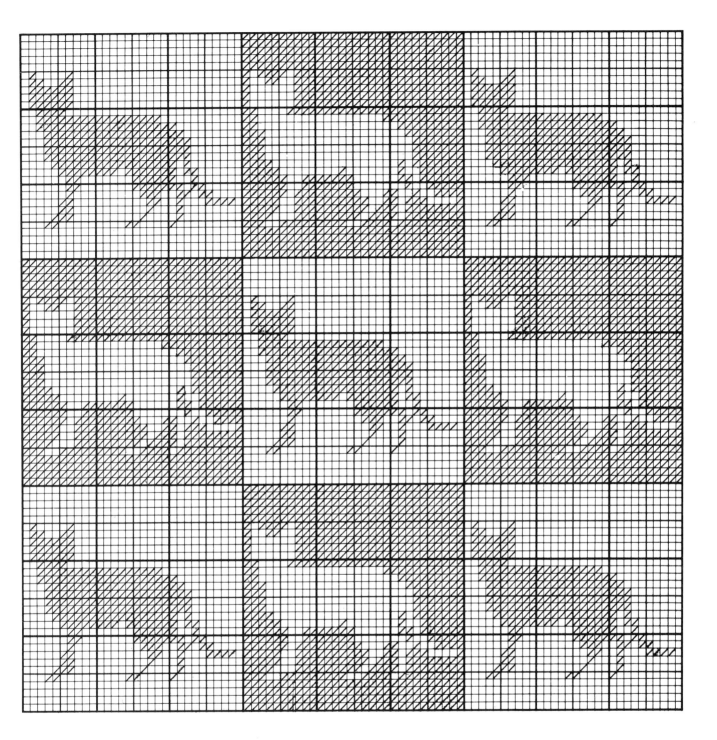

CHECKERBOARD

Use color desired.

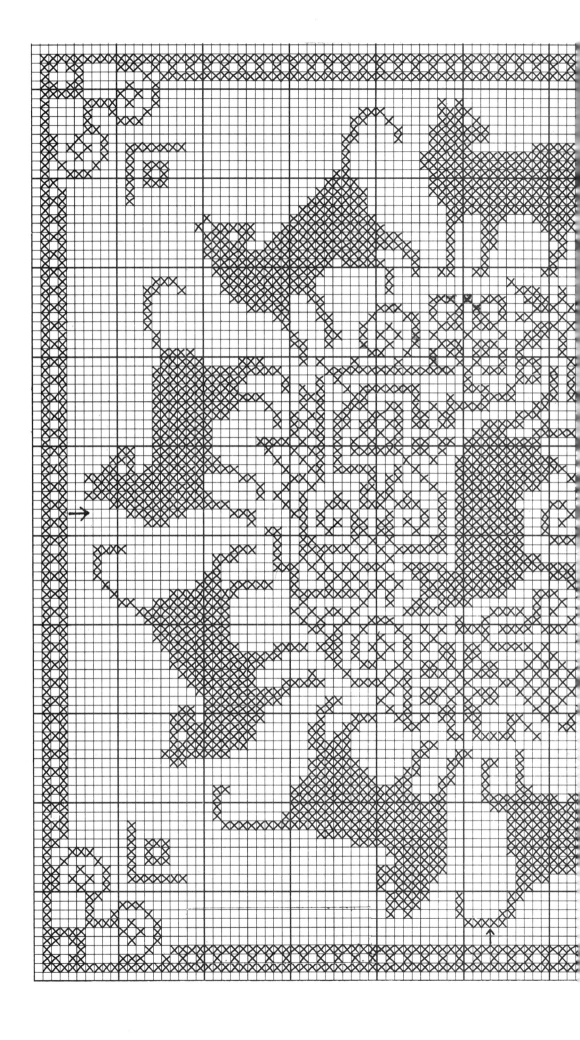

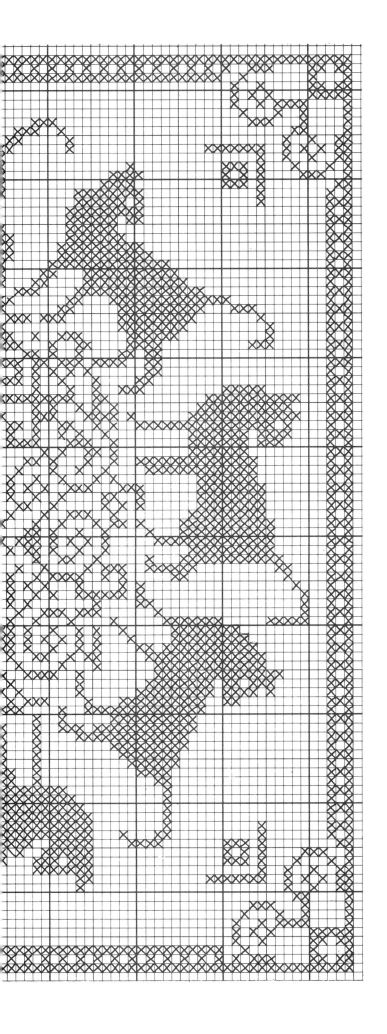

EGYPTIAN CATS

(See color illustration on inside back cover.)

DMC #

☐ 822   *Light Beige Gray for background

☒ 839   Dark Beige Brown

*For cross-stitch, use light beige gray fabric and
leave the background stitches unworked.

43

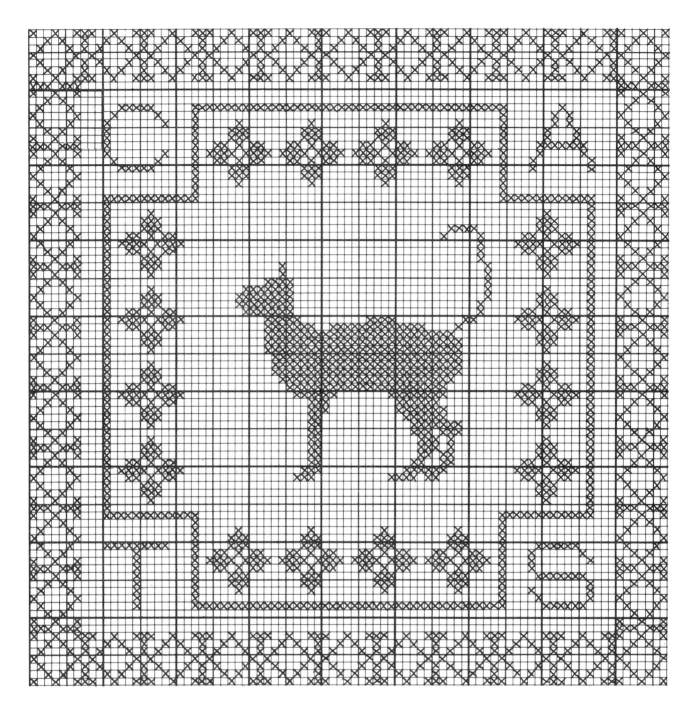

C·A·T·S

(See color illustration on inside front cover.)

Work cat and letters in 823 Dark Navy Blue
and border in 304 Medium Christmas Red.

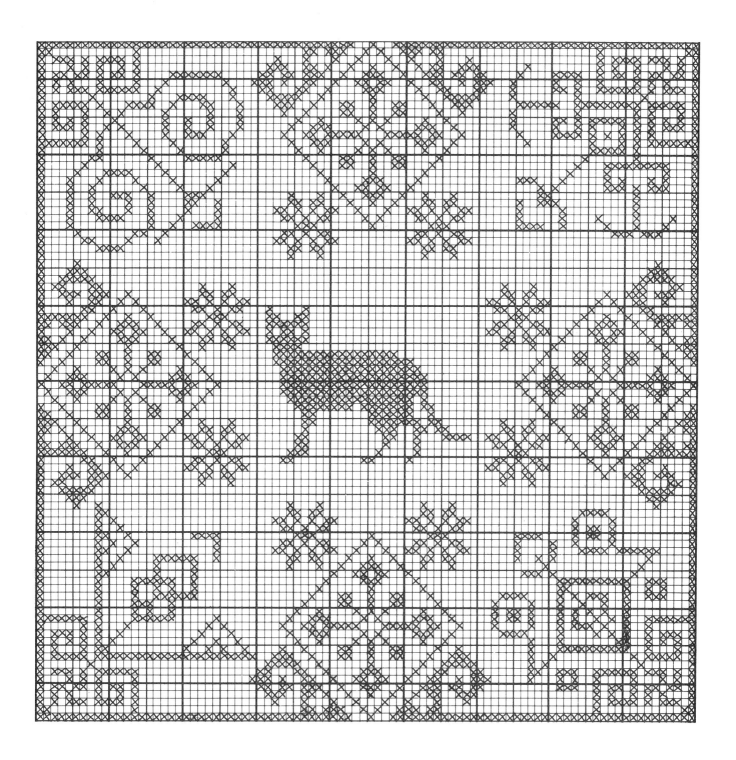

CRYSTALS

(See color illustration on back cover.)

954 Nile Green for all stitches or use color desired.

SITTING PRETTY

(See color illustration on inside front cover.)

311 Medium Navy Blue for all stitches
or use color desired.

NINE LIVES

(See color illustration on inside back cover.)

Work cats in 839 Dark Beige Brown and numbers,
letters and borders in 742 Light Tangerine.